READING LEVEL: 3 / INTEREST LEVEL: 2-5

TITLE	PRINT ISBN	eBOOK ISBN	©	GRL	DEWEY	ATOS
BUY ALL (54 titles)	978-1-5026-5316-1					
GROUP 9						
Cuba (Laura L. Sullivan)	978-1-5026-5174-7	978-1-5026-5175-4	©2020	P	972.91	PENDING
El Salvador (Alicia Z. Klepeis)	978-1-5026-5166-2	978-1-5026-5167-9	©2020	P	972.84	PENDING
Haiti (Joanne Mattern)	978-1-5026-5178-5	978-1-5026-5179-2	©2020	P	972.94	PENDING
Poland (Joanne Mattern)	978-1-5026-5158-7	978-1-5026-5159-4	©2020	Q	943.8	PENDING
Romania (Laura L. Sullivan)	978-1-5026-5162-4	978-1-5026-5163-1	©2020	Q	949.8	PENDING
Switzerland (Alicia Z. Klepeis)	978-1-5026-5170-9	978-1-5026-5171-6	©2020	R	949.4	PENDING
GROUP 8	978-1-5026-4758-0					
Chile (Alicia Z. Klepeis)	978-1-5026-4708-5	978-1-5026-4709-2	©2020	P	983	
Colombia (Alicia Z. Klepeis)	978-1-5026-4712-2	978-1-5026-4713-9	©2020	P	986.1	
Hungary (Joanne Mattern)	978-1-5026-4728-3	978-1-5026-4729-0	©2020	Q	943.9	
Sri Lanka (Laura L. Sullivan)	978-1-5026-4720-7	978-1-5026-4721-4	©2020	R	954.93	
Thailand (Joanne Mattern)	978-1-5026-4724-5	978-1-5026-4725-2	©2020	R	959.3	
Venezuela (Laura L. Sullivan)	978-1-5026-4716-0	978-1-5026-4717-7	©2020	Q	987	
GROUP 7	978-1-5026-4376-6					
Argentina (Joanne Mattern)	978-1-5026-4317-9	978-1-5026-4318-6	©2019	P	982	
Indonesia (Alicia Z. Klepeis)	978-1-5026-4336-0	978-1-5026-4337-7	©2019	P	959.8	
Japan (Joanne Mattern)	978-1-5026-4340-7	978-1-5026-4341-4	©2019	Q	952	
Malaysia (Laura L. Sullivan)	978-1-5026-4344-5	978-1-5026-4345-2	©2019	R	959.5	
Myanmar (Laura L. Sullivan)	978-1-5026-4348-3	978-1-5026-4349-0	©2019	R	959.1	
Singapore (Alicia Z. Klepeis)	978-1-5026-4356-8	978-1-5026-4357-5	©2019	R	959.57	

* See back for more! ⟹

Library Binding • 32 pp. • 7 1/8" x 8 1/2" • Full-Color Photographs and Illustrations • Fact Boxes • Further Information Section
Glossary • Index • Maps • Sidebars • Websites

Each Book: $29.93/**$20.95**/$18.86 (with EAP) • 6-Book Set: $179.58/**$125.70**/$113.16 (with EAP) • Buy All (54 titles); $1616.22/**$1131.30**

EXPLORING WORLD CULTURES

Poland

Joanne Mattern

Cavendish
Square

New York

Published in 2020 by Cavendish Square Publishing, LLC
243 5th Avenue, Suite 136, New York, NY 10016

Copyright © 2020 by Cavendish Square Publishing, LLC

First Edition

Library of Congress Cataloging-in-Publication Data

Names: Mattern, Joanne, 1963- author.
Title: Poland / Joanne Mattern.
Description: First edition. | New York : Cavendish Square, [2020] | Series: Exploring world cultures | Includes bibliographical references and index. | Audience: Grades 2-5.
Identifiers: LCCN 2019016375 (print) | LCCN 2019016916 (ebook) | ISBN 9781502651594 (ebook) | ISBN 9781502651587 (library bound) | ISBN 9781502651563 (pbk.) | ISBN 9781502651570 (6 pack)
Subjects: LCSH: Poland--Juvenile literature.
Classification: LCC DK4147 (ebook) | LCC DK4147 .M38 2020 (print) | DDC 943.8--dc23
LC record available at https://lccn.loc.gov/2019016375

Editor: Lauren Miller
Copy Editor: Nathan Heidelberger
Associate Art Director: Alan Sliwinski
Designer: Christina Shults
Production Coordinator: Karol Szymczuk
Photo Research: J8 Media

The photographs in this book are used by permission and through the courtesy of:
Cover David Grossman/Alamy Stock Photo; p 5 Ewg3D/Getty Images; p. 6 Pavelena/Shutterstock.com; p. 7 Alex Ugalek/Shutterstock.com; p. 8 Prachaya Roekdeethaweesab/Shutterstock.com; p. 9 Szymon Kaczmarczyk/Shutterstock.com; p. 10 Mateusz Slodkowski/SOPA Images/LightRocket/Getty Images; p. 11 Georges De Keerle/Getty Images; p. 12 Beata Zawrzel/NurPhoto/Getty Images; p. 13 Przemek Tokar/Shutterstock.com; p. 14 Vital Severny/Shutterstock.com; p. 15 Kamil Kurus/Shutterstock.com; p. 16 Steve Skjold/Alamy Stock Photo; p. 18 Huw Jones/Lonely Planet Images/Getty Images; p. 19 Caiaimage/Rafal Rodzoch/Getty Images; p. 20 Agencja Fotograficzna Caro/Alamy Stock Photo; p. 21 Vittoriano Rastelli/Corbis/Getty Images; p. 22 MircoV/Shutterstock.com; p. 24 VStock/Alamy Stock Photo; p. 26 Dziurek/Shutterstock.com; p. 27 NurPhoto/NurPhoto/Getty Images; p. 28 Brent Hofacker/Shutterstock.com; p. 29 Vivooo/Shutterstock.com.

Printed in the United States of America

Contents

Introduction

Poland is a country in Eastern Europe. This nation has a beautiful countryside. There are many lakes, and the land is mostly flat. Poland is home to many different plants and animals. There are also busy, crowded cities with beautiful old buildings and modern ones.

Most of Poland is surrounded by other countries. In the north, it borders the Baltic Sea. More than thirty-eight million people live in Poland. These people are called Poles. Poland is the eighth-largest country in Europe.

Poland has faced many difficult times in its long history. It has been ruled by kings and **communists**. Its people have suffered through wars and hard times. Like people everywhere, though, the Polish people still know how to enjoy life. They work, but they also play sports and appreciate the arts. They share delicious meals too. Let's explore the interesting country of Poland!

Old buildings line a cobblestone street in the Old Town part of Warsaw, which is the capital of Poland.

Poland is a large European country. It covers 120,726 square miles (312,679 square kilometers). It has seven neighbors. Ukraine, Belarus, Lithuania, and a small part of Russia lie to the east. Germany lies to the west. The Czech Republic and Slovakia are south of Poland.

Poland has many cities.

FACT!

The highest mountain in Poland is Mount Rysy. It is 8,199 feet (2,499 meters) tall. It is located on the border of Poland and Slovakia.

Mild Weather

Poland has a temperate climate. This means that it is not too hot in the summer or too cold in the winter. However, it is very chilly in the mountains.

Snow covers this Polish mountain.

Along with the Baltic Sea to the north, Poland has many other waterways. The country has more than nine thousand lakes. The largest lakes are Śniardwy, Łebsko, Drawsko, and Mamry.

Most of Poland is flat. The Carpathian Mountains lie on the country's southeastern border. Another mountain range, called the Sudeten, crosses southern Poland.

People have lived in Poland for a long time. During the 600s CE, tribes called the Slavs came to Poland from other parts of Europe and Asia. One famous ruler was Mieszko I. He helped Poland become a large and powerful nation.

This picture of Mieszko I is on Polish money.

In 1569, the Polish-Lithuanian Commonwealth was created. There were many arguments over how to run this government. It lasted until 1795. Later, Poland became a **democratic republic**.

FACT!

Poland is named after a Slavic tribe called the Polan.

In 1939, the German army invaded Poland. This started World War II. During this war, millions of people, including Jewish people, were sent to **concentration camps** in Poland.

After the war, Russia took control of Poland. The nation became a communist country. In 1989, the communist government fell. Now, Poland is a free society.

Auschwitz

During World War II, more than one million people died at a Polish concentration camp called Auschwitz. Today, Auschwitz is a museum.

This is Auschwitz's main gate.

Today, Poland is a democratic republic. The government is split into three parts: executive, legislative, and judicial. The president and the prime minister make up

Poland's prime minister talks to officials in 2019.

the executive part. The president does not have much power. The prime minister is the leader of the country. He or she chooses people to lead different departments.

FACT!

In 1596, Warsaw became Poland's capital city. About 1.8 million people live there today.

A Polish Hero

In the 1980s, Lech Wałęsa led a Polish political group called Solidarity. They fought against communist rule. When communism fell in 1989, Wałęsa became Poland's president.

This photo shows Lech Wałęsa in 1990.

The parliament makes up the legislative part. It is split into two groups, the Senate and the Sejm. They make Poland's laws. Both groups have to approve laws for them to become official.

The judicial part interprets Poland's laws for its people. It is made up of courts. The most important court in Poland is the Supreme Court.

When communism ended in 1989, Poland's **economy** was in bad shape. The new democratic government worked hard to make it stronger.

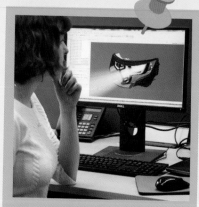

A woman works at a light technology company in Poland.

Today, Polish people work in many industries. Some are teachers, bankers, and public transportation workers. Others have jobs in offices,

FACT!

Poland is one of the largest producers of amber. This golden material is used to make jewelry.

Polish Money

Polish money is called the zloty. The money comes in different colors and sizes depending on how much it is worth.

Zlotys honor many important Poles.

stores, and hotels. Many companies from other countries have offices located in Poland.

Lots of things are made in Poland. Factories make machinery, ships, cars, furniture, glass, and cloth. Mining is also important. Poland's mines produce copper, silver, coal, and iron.

About 10 percent of Poland's people work in farming. They grow wheat, potatoes, oats, and barley. Dairy farms produce milk and cheese. Farmers also raise chickens, pigs, and cattle.

In the past, most of Poland was covered with forests. However, many of those trees were cut down. Today, there are small forests left. They are made up of pine, spruce, elm, willow, and oak trees. During the summer, wildflowers like poppies, crocuses, and flax bloom.

A stork perches high in a tree.

Many different animals live in Poland. Hundreds of birds live here or travel here to lay their eggs. Many areas where birds build nests

FACT!

The red poppy flower is a symbol of Poland.

14

are protected by law. Large animals like brown bears, deer, elk, and bison also live here. Smaller animals do too. These include foxes, lynx, rabbits, and wild hamsters.

Pond turtles are found all over Poland's waterways.

Poland's rivers and lakes are filled with fish like trout, pike, and perch. The Baltic Sea is home to herring, cod, and jellyfish.

Creepy Crawlers

There are many frogs that live in Poland, but only four kinds of snakes and four kinds of lizards live here.

Before World War II, many different **ethnic** groups lived in Poland. During the war, many groups were killed or forced to move to other places. That's because a German leader named Adolf Hitler believed that

A Polish family enjoys an outdoor picnic.

Aryan people were better than everyone else. He had soldiers kidnap and kill many people who were not Aryan. Some people escaped. They

FACT!

The average Polish person lives to be seventy-eight years old.

Silesian Independence

Some Silesians would like to become an independent nation. This new country would include parts of present-day Poland, Germany, and the Czech Republic.

went to other countries. Today, about 97 percent of Poland's people are ethnically Polish.

Besides the Polish, the largest ethnic group is the Silesians. These people are both Polish and German. They live in southwestern Poland. Another group called the Kashubians lives in the north near the Baltic Sea. Other Europeans like Germans, Ukrainians, and Belarusians also live in Poland.

Lifestyle

Many Poles live in cities. Warsaw is the largest city and also the capital of Poland. Other big cities are Kraków, Gdańsk, Wrocław, and Łódź. These cities are crowded, so people live in apartments instead of houses. They travel by train, bus, or car.

Shoppers explore Kraków's Main Market Square.

In other parts of Poland, there are small villages. People live in houses with yards. People

FACT!

Jagiellonian University is the oldest university in Poland. It was founded in Kraków in 1364.

Staying Healthy

Polish people pay taxes. The government uses part of this money to pay for health care for everyone in Poland.

Poland offers citizens free health care.

from the city like to go to the countryside on weekends and holidays to enjoy nature's beauty. They also enjoy visiting Poland's national parks.

Polish children start school at six years old. When they are fourteen, students can go to high school or **vocational** school. Many students go to college after high school.

Religion

Religion is very important in Poland. Almost everyone in Poland is Roman Catholic. Catholicism has been the largest religion in Poland for hundreds of years.

People attend a Mass at a Catholic church in Kraków.

There are other religious groups in Poland. There are Protestant and Eastern Orthodox Christians. Smaller groups

FACT!

People in Poland have religious freedom. They can follow any religion they want.

of Muslims, Pentecostals, Jehovah's Witnesses, and Seventh-Day Adventists are also found in Poland.

Before World War II, about three million Jewish people lived in Poland. During the war, most of them were sent to concentration camps and killed. Today, there are less than ten thousand Jewish people in Poland. Most of them live in Warsaw.

The Polish Pope

In 1978, Cardinal Karol Wojtyła became Pope John Paul II. He was the first non-Italian pope in more than 450 years. Pope John Paul II changed Poland and the world.

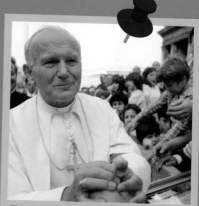

Poland's Pope John Paul II was admired by many.

Language

Polish is spoken in Poland and in other countries around the world. Polish has different styles, or dialects. A dialect called Lesser Polish is spoken in southern Poland. Greater Polish is spoken in the

A mother and child share a Polish storybook. Many Poles love to read.

west. In eastern and central Poland, people speak Mazovian. Silesian is spoken in the southwest.

FACT!

The Goral people in southern Poland speak their own Polish dialect.

A Separate Language

Silesians are proud of their language. They do not think of Silesian as a Polish dialect. Instead, they say it is its own language, even though it shares similarities with Polish.

The Polish alphabet has thirty-two letters. There are twenty-three consonants and nine vowels. Most of the letters are the same as in the English alphabet. However, the letters *q*, *v*, and *x* are not part of the Polish alphabet.

Some people in Poland speak other languages too. Many people speak English, which is taught in school. Other common languages include German and Russian.

Polish people celebrate many Catholic holidays. Christmas and Easter are the most important. Christmas is celebrated on December 24, 25, and 26. Families decorate their homes and share a special meal. They also go to church. On Easter, children enjoy painting eggs.

A Polish family decorates a Christmas tree together.

FACT!

On Christmas Eve, Polish people eat twelve dishes to honor the twelve apostles, Jesus's main students.

Art and literature are very important in Polish culture. Religion is an important theme in both art and stories. Poland's struggle for freedom is a common subject too. As of 2019, five Poles have won the Nobel Prize for Literature.

Polish people also enjoy music and dancing. The *mazurka* (mah-ZER-kah) is a popular traditional dance. Another traditional dance is called the *polonaise* (poh-loh-NEZ). Today, Polish musicians play rock, jazz, classical, and folk music.

Making Movies

Many Polish movies show life during World War II or under communism. They often talk about the fight for freedom.

People in Poland enjoy many different sports. The most popular sport is soccer. The nation has several professional teams. Both adults and children enjoy playing at school or in public parks. Basketball and volleyball are also popular sports.

Motorcycles zoom around the track in a speedway race.

FACT!

Polish children enjoy a game called *zośka* (ZOY-shkah). They pass a ball back and forth using any body part except their hands.

26

An Olympic Queen

Cross-country skier Justyna Kowalczyk's nickname is Queen Justyna. She won five Olympic medals in three different Olympics, including gold medals in 2010 and 2014.

champion skier Justyna Kowalczyk

Many people enjoy motorcycle racing. The most important kind of racing is called speedway. Motorcycles race around a dirt track. The cycles have no brakes. It is dangerous but exciting.

With so many lakes and rivers in Poland, many people enjoy water sports like swimming and kayaking. In the Baltic Sea, some people go scuba diving. The mountains in southern Poland are great for skiing and hiking.

Food

Polish food includes lots of meat and vegetables. Kielbasa (keel-BAH-sah) is a popular sausage. It can be made of beef, pork, chicken, turkey, or lamb. Poles eat it in a bun like a hot dog, slice it up, or put it in soup.

Cherry filling oozes from this tasty *paczki*.

Pierogies (pih-ROH-gees) are another popular food. These dumplings can be filled with meat,

FACT!

Tea is a very popular drink in Poland. Many Poles drink black tea at every meal.

Polish Pancakes

Polish pancakes are called *polskie naleśniki* (POHL-shkey NAH-leh-SHNEE-key). They are very thin and topped with things like cheese, fruit, meat, or vegetables.

Powdered sugar tops these Polish pancakes.

cheese, potatoes, or vegetables. In the past, only poor people ate pierogies. Today, they are enjoyed by everyone.

Polish desserts are sweet! One of the most popular desserts is a kind of donut called *paczki* (POHN-sh-key). They are filled with jam, chocolate, or cream. Cheesecake, poppy seed cake, and cookies made of fried dough are also popular.

Glossary

Aryan — A race of white people, usually with blond hair and blue eyes.

communists — People in a government where all property is owned by the state.

concentration camps — Places where Jewish people were sent to live and work during World War II. Many people died there.

democratic republic — A nation where the people vote for who should run the government.

economy — The use of money to buy and sell goods in a country.

ethnic — Relating to people who have a common national or cultural tradition.

vocational — Relating to a specialized skill such as woodworking or engineering.

Find Out More

Books

Mara, Wil. *Poland*. New York, NY: Scholastic, 2014.

Walser, David. *The Glass Mountain: Tales from Poland*.
Somerville, MA: Candlewick Press, 2014.

Website

National Geographic Kids: Poland

kids.nationalgeographic.com/explore/countries/

poland/#poland-warsaw.jpg

Video

10 Facts About Poland

www.youtube.com/watch?v=kSPznjX8t0w

This video provides viewers with fun facts

about Poland.

Index

About the Author

Joanne Mattern is the author of more than 250 books for children. She specializes in writing nonfiction and has explored many different places in her writing. Her favorite topics include history, travel, sports, biography, and animals. Mattern lives in New York State with her husband, four children, and several pets.